Holidays and Celebrations
Christmas

by Brenda Haugen

illustrated by Todd Ouren

Thanks to our advisers for their expertise, research, and advice:

Alexa Sandmann, Ed.D., Professor of Literacy
The University of Toledo, Toledo, Ohio
Member, National Council for the Social Studies

Susan Kesselring, M.A., Literacy Educator
Rosemount-Apple Valley-Eagan (Minnesota) School District

PICTURE WINDOW BOOKS
MINNEAPOLIS, MINNESOTA

For Nicole, the greatest gift in my life

Managing Editor: Bob Temple
Creative Director: Terri Foley
Editor: Sara E. Hoffmann
Editorial Adviser: Andrea Cascardi
Copy Editor: Laurie Kahn
Designer: Melissa Voda
Page production: The Design Lab
The illustrations in this book were rendered digitally.

Picture Window Books
5115 Excelsior Boulevard
Suite 232
Minneapolis, MN 55416
1-877-845-8392
www.picturewindowbooks.com

Printed in the United States of America.

Library of Congress Cataloging-in-Publication Data
Haugen, Brenda.
Christmas / written by Brenda Haugen ; illustrated by Todd Ouren.
p. cm. — (Holidays and celebrations)
Summary: Briefly discusses the history and customs connected to the celebration
of Christmas. Includes bibliographical references.
ISBN 1-4048-0192-8
1. Christmas—Juvenile literature. [1. Christmas. 2. Holidays.] I. Ouren, Todd, ill.
II. Title. III. Holidays and celebrations (Picture Window Books)
GT4985.5 .H38 2004
394.2663--dc21
2003006107

The big jolly man in the bright red suit brings presents. The children sing pretty Christmas songs.

Santa

4

People wrap packages
with colorful bows.

Songs about jingle bells
play on the radio.
It's Christmastime!

Christmas is a time of great joy.
People sing carols and eat sweet treats.

Children hang stockings. They hope their stockings will be filled with fun gifts.

Many treats are traditional at Christmas. Candy canes and gingerbread are traditional sweets.

Do you know why people
celebrate Christmas?

Christmas is a Christian holiday.
It celebrates the birth of Jesus Christ.

Jesus Christ was born about 2,000 years ago. Christians believe Jesus is the son of God.

9

Christmas includes even older traditions, too.

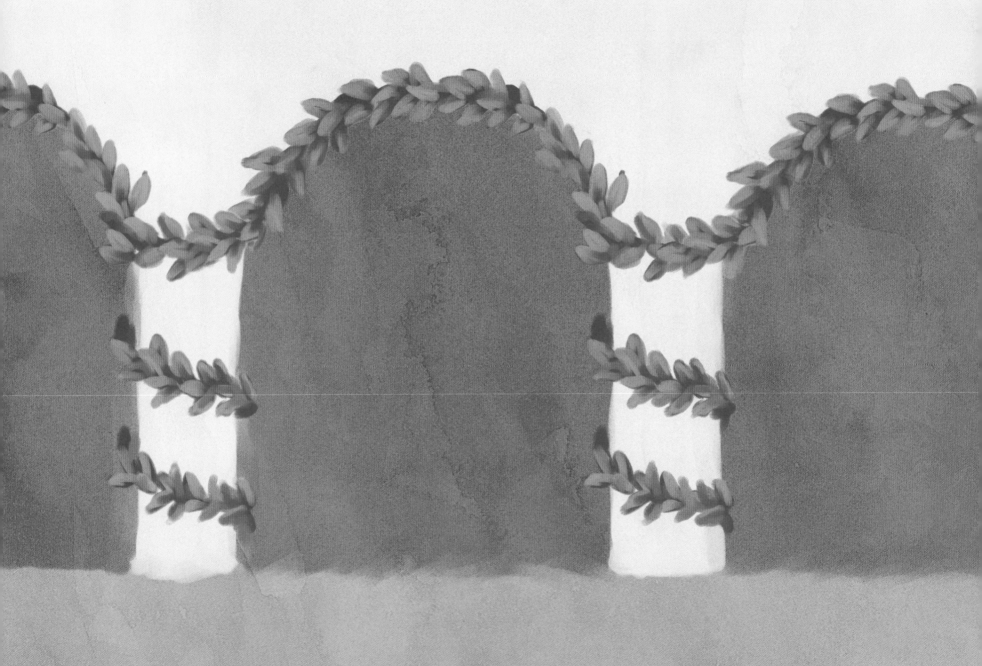

People once celebrated the changing seasons. The celebrations became part of Christmas tradition.

Around Christmastime, the sun sets early. There is less daylight than in the summer.

Long ago, Romans put lights in their windows on dark days. They thought this would bring back the sun.

Today, people decorate their homes with lights.

Other ancient people decorated evergreen trees. They once believed the pretty trees would make the sun return.

Today, people decorate evergreens with sparkly lights and colored balls. Decorated trees are symbols of Christmas. Stars and angels are Christmas symbols, too.

Germans brought the tradition of Christmas trees to the United States when they settled there in the 1800s.

15

At Christmastime, families and friends like to gather.

When people get together at Christmas, they often bring gifts for one another. They put the presents under the Christmas tree.

Who else brings Christmas gifts?
He's big and jolly and wears a red suit.
It must be Santa Claus!

Children send letters to Santa
at the North Pole. If the children
are good, Santa fills their stockings
with gifts on Christmas Eve.

Santa isn't the only
one who gets lots
of mail at Christmastime.
People send millions
of Christmas cards
every year.

Enjoy the Christmas season.
Give a gift to someone special.
Eat a candy cane, and sing
a Christmas carol.

Remember why people celebrate Christmas, and keep joy in your heart all year long.

You Can Make a Candy Picture Frame

What you need:

tacky glue

jumbo craft sticks

small bag of round, wrapped peppermints

scissors

cardboard

a special photograph (Ask your parents for permission first.) You also
can draw a picture of your family or friends to put in your frame.

What you do:

1. Make sure you have an adult to help you.
2. Glue four craft sticks together to make a square.
   This square will be your frame.
3. On the front of your frame, glue the peppermints along the edge.
   Don't take the wrappers off the peppermints.
4. Cut the cardboard so that it is a little bit smaller than the outside edge
   of your frame.
5. Cut the picture to fit inside your frame.
6. Glue the picture to the center of the cardboard.
7. Glue the cardboard to the back of the frame. Make sure the picture
   is facing the right way.

Fun Facts

- Many Christians go to church at midnight on Christmas Eve. A special service is held in the city of Bethlehem at that time, too. Jesus was born in Bethlehem.

- Long ago, a wealthy man named Nicholas passed out gifts to children and the poor. He kept his good deeds a secret. This is why Santa Claus also is called St. Nicholas.

- In Poland, people have a special Christmas Eve meal. They eat sauerkraut, fish, potato pancakes, and beet soup.

- After a trip to Mexico, a man named Joel Poinsett brought back a beautiful red and green plant to America. These plants became popular at Christmastime. People began calling them poinsettias.

- People started sending Christmas cards nearly 200 years ago!

- In Scandinavia, children leave their shoes by their fireplaces. They hope St. Nicholas will fill their shoes with treats on Christmas Eve.

Words to Know

carol—a joyful song, especially one that people sing at Christmastime

Christian—a person who follows the teachings of Jesus Christ

season—one of the four parts of the year—winter, spring, summer, or autumn

symbol—something that stands for something else

tradition—a belief or custom handed down to children from their parents

wealthy—having lots of money

To Learn More

At the Library

dePaola, Tomie. **The Legend of the Poinsettia**. New York: Putnam, 1994.

Hintz, Martin. **Christmas: Why We Celebrate It the Way We Do**. Mankato, Minn.: Capstone Press, 1996.

Rau, Dana Meachen. **Christmas**. New York: Children's Press, 2000.

Roberts, Bethany. **Christmas Mice!** New York: Clarion Books, 2000.

Sabuda, Robert. **The Christmas Alphabet**. New York: Orchard Books, 1994.

Fact Hound

Fact Hound offers a safe, fun way to find Web sites related to this book. All of the sites on Fact Hound have been researched by our staff.
http://www.facthound.com

1. Visit the Fact Hound home page.
2. Enter a search word related to this book, or type in this special code: 1404801928.
3. Click on the FETCH IT button.

Your trusty Fact Hound will fetch the best sites for you!

Index